BOOKWORMS

Creepy Crawlers

Spiders

Jack K. Patterson

I0808604

Cavendish Square
New York

Published in 2019 by Cavendish Square Publishing, LLC
243 5th Avenue, Suite 136, New York, NY 10016

Copyright © 2019 by Cavendish Square Publishing, LLC

First Edition

No part of this publication may be reproduced, stored in a retrieval system, or transmitted in any form or by any means—electronic, mechanical, photocopying, recording, or otherwise—without the prior permission of the copyright owner. Request for permission should be addressed to Permissions, Cavendish Square Publishing, 243 5th Avenue, Suite 136, New York, NY 10016. Tel (877) 980-4450; fax (877) 980-4454.

Website: cavendishsq.com

This publication represents the opinions and views of the author based on his or her personal experience, knowledge, and research. The information in this book serves as a general guide only. The author and publisher have used their best efforts in preparing this book and disclaim liability rising directly or indirectly from the use and application of this book.

All websites were available and accurate when this book was sent to press.

Library of Congress Cataloging-in-Publication Data

Names: Patterson, Jack K., 1988- author.
Title: Spiders / Jack K. Patterson.
Description: First edition. | New York : Cavendish Square, 2019. | Series: Creepy crawlers | Audience: Grades K-3. | Includes index.
Identifiers: LCCN 2018024023 (print) | LCCN 2018025455 (ebook) | ISBN 9781502642820 (ebook) |
ISBN 9781502642691 (library bound) | ISBN 9781502642806 (paperback) | ISBN 9781502642813 (6 pack)
Subjects: LCSH: Spiders--Juvenile literature.
Classification: LCC QL458.4 (ebook) | LCC QL458.4 .P385 2019 (print) | DDC 595.4/4--dc23
LC record available at https://lccn.loc.gov/2018024023

Editorial Director: David McNamara
Editor: Kristen Susienka
Copy Editor: Nathan Heidelberger
Associate Art Director: Alan Sliwinski
Designer: Megan Metté
Production Coordinator: Karol Szymczuk
Photo Research: J8 Media

The photographs in this book are used by permission and through the courtesy of: Cover James van den Broek/Shutterstock.com; p. 5 Aleksey Stemmer/Shutterstock.com; p. 7 Marek Mierzejewski/Shutterstock.com; p. 9 Paula French/Shutterstock.com; p. 11 Antje Schulte/Spiders and Co./Alamy Stock Photo; p. 13 Ketnarong/Shutterstock.com; p. 15 Thomas Males/Shutterstock.com; p. 17 Vsb Viveksharma/Shutterstock.com; p. 19 Amy Johansson/Shutterstock.com; p. 21 Kseniya Lanzarote/Shutterstock.com.

Printed in the United States of America

Contents

Spiders have eight long legs and small black eyes.

They look creepy!

A spider starts life inside an egg.

The egg is in an egg **sac**.

One egg sac holds many eggs.

Soon the eggs **hatch**.

A baby spider is called a spiderling.

Spiderlings look like small adult spiders.

Spiderlings leave their homes to find new ones.

They do this by **ballooning**.

Ballooning is when the wind carries them away.

Adult spiders can be big or small.

Most spiders are gray, brown, or black.

Some spiders have bright colors on them.

Bright colors warn **predators** to stay away.

Spiders live all over the world.

Some spiders live in deserts, forests, or jungles.

Many spiders make a web.

A web is made of spider silk.

Spiders catch insects in
a web.

Insects are a spider's food.

Spiders might look creepy.

But they are fun to
learn about.

What do you like most
about spiders?

New Words

ballooning (ball-OON-ing) When a baby spider leaves home. It makes a strand of silk and lets the wind carry it away to another place.

hatch (HATCH) When a baby spider breaks through an egg.

predators (PRED-uh-torz) Animals or insects that want to eat other animals or insects.

sac (SAK) A bag or pouch that holds spider eggs. Spiders make egg sacs from silk.

Index

About the Author

Jack K. Patterson lives in Boston, Massachusetts. He enjoys gardening, bird watching, and exploring the outdoors. He is an insect enthusiast who has his own bug collection. He enjoys learning about the world around him.

About BOOKWORMS

Bookworms help independent readers gain reading confidence through high-frequency words, simple sentences, and strong picture/text support. Each book explores a concept that helps children relate what they read to the world they live in.